HAIR!

ANIMAL FUR, WOOL, AND MORE

MARILYN SINGER

ILLUSTRATIONS BY JULIE COLOMBET

M MILLBROOK PRESS · MINNEAPOLIS

To Kym Prager-Wilson, who knows
a lot about hair —M.S.

Many thanks to Steve Aronson and to my editors, Carol Hinz and
Shaina Olmanson, and the other good folks at Lerner Publishing

Millbrook Press
A division of Lerner Publishing Group, Inc.
241 First Avenue North
Minneapolis, MN 55401 USA

For reading levels and more information, look up this title at www.lernerbooks.com.

Designed by Emily Harris.
Main body text set in Mikado Medium 13/18.
Typeface provided by HVD Fonts.
The illustrations in this book were created with pencil with digitally added color.

Library of Congress Cataloging-in-Publication Data

Names: Singer, Marilyn, author. | Colombet, Julie, illustrator.
Title: Hair! : animal fur, wool, and more / by Marilyn Singer ; illustrated by Julie Colombet.
Description: Minneapolis : Millbrook Press, [2019] | Audience: Age 7–12. | Audience: Grade 4
    to 6. | Includes bibliographical references.
Identifiers: LCCN 2018022632 (print) | LCCN 2018032786 (ebook) | ISBN 9781541543799
    (eb pdf) | ISBN 9781512449150 (lb : alk. paper)
Subjects: LCSH: Hair—Juvenile literature. | Fur—Juvenile literature.
Classification: LCC QL942 (ebook) | LCC QL942 .S56168 2019 (print) | DDC 591.47—dc23

LC record available at https://lccn.loc.gov/2018022632

Manufactured in the United States of America
1-42847-26511-9/12/2018

Were you a hairy baby? When you were born, did you have a head full of curls or straight locks? Or were you as bald as a melon?

You think *that's* hairy?

How about *before* you were born? Were you hairy then?

Yes! Whether or not you had hair on your head, before you were born, you had a mustache. That mustache spread all over your body, turning into fine hair known as **lanugo.** It combined with a waxy coating to protect your skin from the fluid you were floating in. Lanugo usually disappears before babies are born, but sometimes it takes a few days or even weeks before it disappears completely.

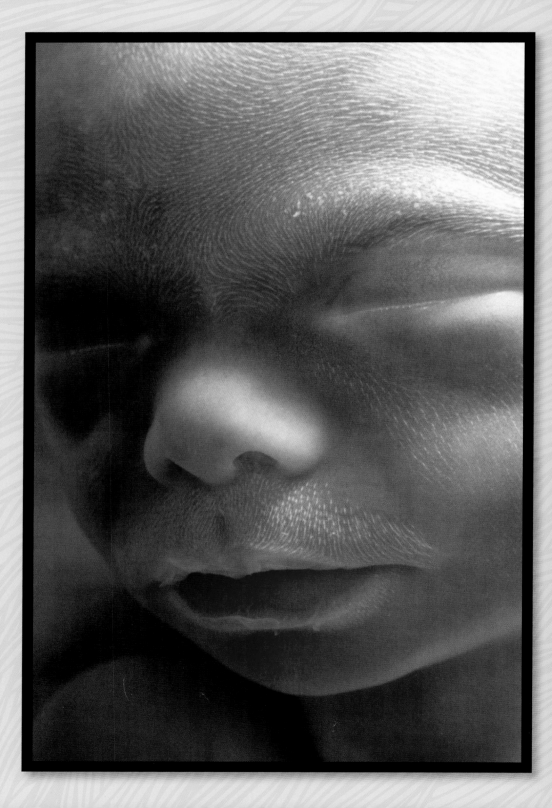

As you got older, you grew other kinds of hair, some of it finer and some of it thicker. It means one important thing: you are a **mammal!**

Am I a mammal too?

No, silly. You've got feathers, not hair.

Only mammals have hair. But different mammals have different types of hair. Look at your family and friends. All of their bodies are covered with hair. Some of them have a lot more hair than others. But even hairy people are not nearly as hairy as most other mammals. Watch a show about animals in the Arctic, take a trip to the zoo, or just look at the dogs in your neighborhood and you'll see some really hairy critters. You'll also see that hair comes in different forms, colors, and textures. It can be straight, wavy, or curly. It can be blond, red, brown, black, gray, and other shades. These forms, colors, and textures are inherited. You, your dog, and that polar bear or tiger at the zoo all get their type of hair from **genes**.

Jeans?

No, genes!

Genes are pieces of information passed from parents to offspring that shape appearance, abilities, and more.

A mammal's hairy covering is called a coat. Zoologists also use the term **pelage.**

When that hair is fine, soft, short, and dense, we call it **fur.**

When hair is thick and curly and doesn't stop growing, we call it **wool.**

Baby animals are often covered with fuzzy hair called **down.**

Even though we have different names for them, fur, wool, and down are all still forms of hair. They help **insulate** an animal, keeping it warm in cold weather.

Hair can also keep an animal's nest or den warm. Mother rabbits will pluck hair from their bellies and backs to make cozy nests for their babies. Weasels will line their nests with the fur of rabbits, rodents, or other animals they've eaten.

I love the snow!

How long until it's spring?

You have to keep warm too, so why aren't *you* covered with fur? Scientists say that people were once much hairier, but we lost our furry coat probably over a million years ago. No one is sure just when or why.

Having less hair was sometimes a problem. As early humans moved from Africa to colder parts of the planet, they had to stay warm. They needed clothes, as well as blankets and rugs—and some of those things were made from fur.

Over thousands of years, humans have bred or hunted a variety of animals for their fur. Unfortunately, hunting has caused a number of mammals to become endangered or extinct. Some, such as bison, were overhunted for their hides as well as their meat. Tigers, jaguars, cheetahs, minks, otters, several species of foxes, and other animals have been pursued and killed as trophies or turned into expensive fur coats.

Some animals bred for their coats have thrived. In many parts of the world, herds of domesticated mammals are raised for their wool. Sheep, llamas, and alpacas get haircuts in the spring, and their wool is gathered and spun into yarn for clothing and blankets.

What do I need this for? I've got my own coat.

But you look so good in red.

An animal's coat is made up of different types of hair. The inner layer, which is softer and finer, is called the **undercoat, or ground hair.** The top layer is made of longer, coarser **guard hairs.** These hairs protect the undercoat from the weather, such as rain and snow; from wear and tear; and sometimes from enemies. A porcupine's barbed quills are guard hairs. No predator wants a mouthful of porcupine hair!

Looking sharp! Get it?

Uh. No.

Guard hairs create the patterns and colors of an animal's coat. A grizzly bear's guard hairs are silver and gray. They create a grizzled—gray-streaked—appearance, which gives the bear its name.

The striped skunk's glossy, black and white guard hairs warn its enemies: "You see me, right? Back off or you'll be sorry!"

P.U.!

I can't smell a thing.

Most birds can't smell anything.

The white hairs on the underside of a white-tailed deer's tail also serve as a warning—to other deer. When a white-tailed deer spots a threat, it raises its tail like a flag, telling members of its herd to run.

Many mammals, including deer and horses, shed, or **molt**, their longer guard hairs for the summer and then grow back shaggier coats for the winter. Rabbits shed every three months or so. Cats, as your couch will tell you, shed constantly. You shed a lot too, but you probably don't notice it.

I don't shed, I molt!

I'm a type of dog that doesn't shed much.

When some animals shed, their new coats are a different color. One variety of the arctic fox has a brown coat in summer and a white one in winter. So does the snowshoe hare. This coloring acts as **camouflage**, letting the fox or hare blend in with soil and rocks or snow, depending on the season.

Many other mammals use camouflage. A giraffe's patterned coat allows it to blend in with shadows and leaves on the African plains. The spots on a fawn's fur make it hard to see in the woods' dappled sunlight. When a tiger is hunting, its stripes help it hide in tall grass.

A zebra's black and white stripes break up its outline and also make it difficult to spot. For a long time, scientists thought the stripes helped zebras escape from predators such as lions. They believed that when a herd of zebras runs from a lion, the zigzag patterns confuse the hunter's eyes so it can't easily attack a single prey. However, recent studies suggest that the zebra's coloring may not be camouflage against predators. Instead, the stripes may have developed to confuse biting flies, which seem to prefer landing on solid colors rather than stripes.

You might think that helpless babies would need camouflage even more than their parents. **So why are young langur monkeys orange while their parents are gray?**

Orange you glad the baby isn't gray? Get it?

Would you call me orange or fawn?

And why do black-and-white colobus monkey parents have pure white offspring?

Both of these species live in groups. Some scientists think that the babies' bright coloring lets each baby's mother, as well as the other members of the troop, recognize and care for them.

My mother recognized me by my scent!

My mother recognized me by my voice! Cheep, cheep!

What about your most noticeable hair—the stuff on your head? Your hair isn't the same as other mammals' guard hairs or undercoat. It's somewhere in between. It does protect you somewhat from the weather, but you still need a hat or umbrella to stay warm and dry. And it isn't likely to help you warn enemies or hide from them either.

So what *does* our head hair do? Some scientists think that one of its main jobs is to display just how good-looking and healthy you are.

I've never even had a cold!

And I'm very good-looking!

In addition to guarding your eyes from insects, dust, rain, and sweat, your eyelashes and eyebrows show off your looks and personality. Eyelashes highlight your eyes. Eyebrows help you communicate emotions such as anger or surprise. And they help us recognize one another.

Other mammals don't have eyebrows, but they do have brow ridges. Monkeys and dogs can raise and lower these ridges to show how they feel.

Camels, horses, and cattle have long eyelashes to protect their eyes.

Surprise!

A number of mammals use their hair to draw attention to themselves and to attract mates. A male lion's lush, striking mane, which is covered with guard hairs, appeals to lionesses. Several types of male fruit bats court females by flashing white **epaulets**—patches of fur on their shoulders—or white crests on the top of their heads. Even without a fancy mane or epaulets, a full, gleaming coat shows that an animal is healthy—and a healthy animal makes a good mate because it can produce and provide for stronger babies.

Trick or treat!

Just how do mammals keep their coats healthy and clean? Humans bathe and shower. We comb and brush our hair. To keep their fur in good shape, other animals must groom themselves too. Dogs lick their feet and whatever body parts they can reach. Cats are more flexible and can lick themselves all over—often. Sometimes our dogs and cats will even groom us, just as if we were puppies and kittens!

I don't need a bath. I really don't!

I do!

24

Other animals take dips in water or use dirt, sand, mud, or dust to get clean. When a pig rolls in mud, it's not being filthy—it's actually removing bugs and bacteria from its hide. Elephants bathe in water or roll in dirt, and they also take showers, using their trunks to spray water or dust on themselves.

Chimpanzees, other apes, and monkeys practice social grooming—they pick insects, twigs, leaves, and other debris out of one another's fur. This practice is not only good for hygiene, but it also helps the troop **bond**—to build trust and cooperation.

We think of apes, monkeys, horses, cats—large and small—and lots of other animals as hairy. But some mammals don't have much hair at all. Elephants, which live in warm climates, have sparse, wiry hair all over their bodies. This thin coat of hair helps protect an elephant from high temperatures by drawing heat off its body.

Naked mole rats live underground in colonies. They don't need protection from the sun, and when it gets cold, they pile on top of one another to keep warm. They are not totally naked. Mole rats have about one hundred fine hairs on their bodies that help them feel what's around them and guide them in the dark.

Some breeds of dogs and cats such as the Xoloitzcuintli (show-low-eetz-KWEENT-lee), also known as the Mexican Hairless dog, and the sphynx cat have very little hair. The Xolo, as it's nicknamed, is an ancient breed. People have used it as food, as protection against evil spirits, and as a heating pad to soothe tummy, muscle, and joint aches. Breeders mated hairless males and females found in some litters to produce hairless pups and create the breed. The sphynx cat was bred in the 1960s from naturally occurring hairless cats. It is particularly popular among people who love felines but are allergic to the **dander**—loose bits of skin—that cling to a cat's fur.

Breeders did not create hairless dolphins. Over millions of years, as they adapted to life in the water, they lost their fur. To keep them insulated in cold seas, dolphins and other whales developed a layer of fat known as **blubber.** But since they are mammals and all mammals have hair, where's theirs? On their baby faces! Dolphins are born with whiskers on their upper jaws. The whiskers fall out as they get older, leaving **pores**—openings—that can sense electrical energy fields to help them navigate and find prey.

A cat's long whiskers, or **vibrissae**, are hairs that are very sensitive to touch. They help the cat detect obstacles and keep its balance. Rats use their whiskers in much the same way—but they can move theirs faster. A walrus has four hundred to seven hundred vibrissae, which help it search for food in the water. Bats that roost in crevices have vibrissae on their rear ends to help them navigate in tight spaces. Many squirrels have them on their legs so that they can move through trees with ease.

I've got vibrissae too.

I thought you had whiskers.

Same thing, noodle.

Did you know you have vibrissae? They're not on your cheeks, around your mouth, or on your legs or rear end. They're in your nose! They help prevent dust, dirt, and bugs from getting up your nostrils. The hairs in your ears perform a similar task, protecting your ear canal from debris.

Whether or not you were born a hairy baby, your hair will certainly change over time. It may get straighter or curlier. It may get darker. You might decide to cut it, shave it, grow it long, or dye it.

Hair today, gone tomorrow.

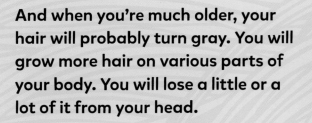

And when you're much older, your hair will probably turn gray. You will grow more hair on various parts of your body. You will lose a little or a lot of it from your head.

If you have children, you may pass your hair's color and texture along to hairy babies of your own.

I get it! Vanishing into thin hair!

Whatever happens with your hair, you should know that no two people—or any other mammals—have hair that's exactly the same. That makes every one of us unique.

Let's get out of hair.

So long! Furwell!

TRIVIAL FURSUIT!

What is hair made of?

Like nails and claws, hair is made of a protein called **keratin**. Each hair grows from a **root**—a group of living cells that produce layers of new cells—from a pit in the skin called a **follicle**. The root produces layers of new cells. These push out the old dead cells, making your hair grow at a rate of about 4 to 6 inches (10 to 15 cm) per year. So the hair you grow is actually dead! That's why it doesn't hurt to get your hair cut.

Even though your hair isn't alive, it still needs to stay healthy. Glands near the follicles produce oil to keep hair soft and shiny. But this oil also makes hair . . . oily. Too much oil and your hair gets dirty and dull and attracts bacteria. That's why you need to wash it to keep it in good condition.

How many hair follicles do we have?

Around 1,000 per square inch (6,450 per sq. cm), which means about 100,000 on our heads and 5 million on our bodies! Men have a few hundred thousand more than women.

> Does it hurt if you pull it?

> Cut that out!

> How many hairs do you have?

> About 15,000 per square inch, so a lot more than 5 million!

Where do humans have NO hair follicles?
On our lips, the palms of our hands, and the soles of our feet.

What animal has the longest hair?
We do! The record for longest hair so far is held by Xie Qiuping from China, whose hair measures more than 18 feet (5.5 m) long.

The wild animal with the longest hair is the musk ox. Its guard hairs can grow 2 feet (0.6 m) long. It needs a warm coat to withstand Arctic temperatures.

What is the hairiest mammal in the world?
Sea otters. A sea otter has eight hundred million to one billion hairs!

What is the softest mammal?
The chinchilla is the softest because fifty or sixty hairs spring from each follicle.

How many hairs do humans normally shed every day?
About one hundred.

I thought you were the hairiest mammal in the world.

Nope. Meet the otter . . .

What causes baldness?

Some people, particularly males, lose much more hair during their lifetimes than other people do. They become bald. Baldness in other animals is almost always caused by disease or parasites. Baldness in people may also be caused by disease and medical treatments, but it's often **genetic**—inherited from our parents.

Which humans have the most head hairs: blonds, brunettes, or redheads?

Blonds! They are born with an average of 150,000 hair follicles. Brunettes have 100,000 to 110,000, and redheads, 90,000.

What gives us our natural hair color?

A group of natural substances in the body called **melanin**. Hair color is genetic. Melanin production decreases with age, and when that happens, mammals—and not just humans—turn gray. Genetics, diseases, medical treatments, and stress affect when an animal's hair begins to turn gray and just how gray it turns.

What animal's fur turns black instead of gray as it ages?

The male giraffe! In older male giraffes, chemical substances in their bodies called **hormones** make their hairy brown blotches turn black.

You're already gray.

And proud of it!

How do we get our hair texture?

Hair texture is created by the shape of the hairs themselves—seen in cross-section, rounded hairs are straighter and flattened hairs are curlier. Like hair color, texture is genetic.

What makes your hair stand on end?

When it's cold, small muscles next to the follicles can make the hairs stand up. In animals with thick coats, this increases insulation. In people, it gives us goose bumps. Humans inherited this reaction from our ancestors, and because we are no longer hairy creatures, goose bumps don't much help us get warmer. We also get goose bumps when we're scared or moved or thrilled. Other mammals raise their hair to look more threatening to their enemies. When a dog raises its **hackles**—the fur on its neck and back—it's sending a message to another dog, person, or being to back off.

How did humans lose their hair?

One theory is that early humans, living on the hot African savannas, lost their hair because they needed to keep cooler. Another interesting theory is that less hair meant fewer nasty parasites—lice, fleas, and ticks—and the diseases they spread.

Ooh, that's pretty scary!

And also pretty hairy!

GLOSSARY

blubber: the thick layer of fat under the skin of sea mammals

bond: to form a trusting, cooperative relationship between members of a group

camouflage: the use of color, light, or material as disguise to blend in with the surroundings

dander: small flakes of skin shed by mammals

down: fuzzy hair that covers baby mammals

epaulets: fancy shoulder decorations

follicle: the tubelike case from which a hair grows

fur: animal hair that is fine, soft, short, and dense

genes: units that determine what features and characteristics are passed on from parents to offspring

genetic: inherited from parents

ground hair: the softer, finer, inner layer of hair, also called the undercoat

guard hairs: top layers of hair that protect from the weather and create animals' colors and patterns

hackles: hairs that stand up on an animal's neck when it is challenged or alarmed

hormones: natural chemical substances in an animal's body that influence its physical functions and behavior

insulate: to use material such as fur to protect from cold, as well as from excess heat

keratin: the key type of protein that makes up hair, horns, hooves, claws, and the outer layer of human skin

lanugo: downy hair that covers the skin of unborn and some newborn babies

mammal: a warm-blooded animal that has hair and provides milk for its young

melanin: natural substances that give hair and skin their color

molt: to shed old hair, feathers, or skin to make way for new growth

pelage: an animal's coat

pores: naturally occurring holes in the surface of an animal's skin

root: a group of living cells that produces layers of new cells

undercoat: the softer, finer inner layer of hair, also called ground hair

vibrissae: long, stiff hairs that are sensitive to touch, known as whiskers

wool: thick, curly hair, especially found on domestic sheep

SELECTED BIBLIOGRAPHY

Armitage, Hanae, and Nala Rogers. "Hair Forensics Could Soon Reveal What You Look Like, Where You've Been." *Science*, March 8, 2016. http://www.sciencemag.org/news /2016/03/hair-forensics-could-soon-reveal-what-you-look -where-you-ve-been.

"Babies Hair." Hairfinder.com. http://www.hairfinder.com /tips/babies_hair.htm.

Bertino, Anthony J., and Patricia Nolan Bertino. "The Study of Hair." Chapter 3 in *Forensic Science: Fundamentals & Investigations*. Mason, OH: South-Western, 2012. http://ngl .cengage.com/assets/downloads/forsci_pro0000000541 /4827_fun_ch3.pdf.

Coffey, Rebecca. "20 Things You Didn't Know about . . . Hair." *Discover*, September 8, 2014. http://discovermagazine.com /2013/may/19-20-things-you-didnt-know-about-hair.

"Hair." New World Encyclopedia. Last modified April 3, 2008. http://www.newworldencyclopedia.org/entry/Hair.

Hutchinson, Sean. "What's the Difference between Hair and Fur?" Mental Floss, October 31, 2014. http://mentalfloss .com/article/58251/whats-difference-between-hair -and-fur.

Lerg, Hayley. "Animal Hair vs Human Hair." Prezi, October 24, 2012. https://prezi.com/zucfmca4ecaw/animal-hair-vs -human-hair/.

McAdams, Molly. "What Is the Function of Human Hair?" Livestrong, July 18, 2017. http://www.livestrong.com /article/76153-function-human-hair/.

Parker, Steve. *Mammal.* London: Dorling Kindersley, 1989.

Tsavliris, Athena. "What You Need to Know about Babies Born with Hair." *Today's Parent*, February 9, 2017. http://www .todaysparent.com/baby/babies-born-with-hair/.

"Types of Hair Fiber." Keratin.com. Accessed September 12, 2018. http://www.keratin.com/aa/aa013.shtml.

Wade, Nicholas. "Why Humans and Their Fur Parted Ways." *New York Times*, August 19, 2003. http://www.nytimes .com/2003/08/19/science/why-humans-and-their-fur -parted-ways.html?pagewanted=all.

Weisberger, Mindy. "Fur, Wool, Hair: What's the Difference?" Live Science, May 11, 2016. https://www.livescience.com /54701-fur-hair-wool-whats-the-difference.html.

FURTHER READING

Books

Markle, Sandra. *What If You Had Animal Hair?* New York: Scholastic, 2014
Readers can imagine themselves with the fur of a polar bear, the quills of a porcupine, or the mane of a lion with this nonfiction title. Each page features facts about an animal and its hair and shows readers what life would be like with it. The end of the book includes a section on hair growth, as well as tips for taking care of human hair.

Silverman, Buffy. *Hair Traits: Color, Texture, and More*. Minneapolis: Lerner Publications, 2013.
This nonfiction book discusses hair as a genetic trait. Readers can learn why some people have curly hair or straight hair and about rare hair traits such as red hair and widow's peaks.

Ward, Jennifer. *Feathers and Hair, What Animals Wear*. New York: Beach Lane Books, 2017.
This picture book gives readers an introductory look at animal body coverings. Informative back matter gives examples of specific animals and shows how their body coverings keep them warm and safe.

Websites

Easy Science for Kids: Hair
http://easyscienceforkids.com/hair/
Did you know that hair grows faster in the summer than in the winter? Or that 95 percent of your body is covered in hair? This website lists fun facts about human hair.

Environmental Education for Kids: Fun Fur Facts
http://eekwi.org/critter/mammal/fur.htm
This site contains fun facts about mammal hair types, as well as information about animal hair color.

Kiddle Encyclopedia: Hair Facts
https://kids.kiddle.co/Hair
Learn all about hair from this children's encyclopedia entry. Topics include hair functions, the genetics and chemistry of hair, and a gallery of images.

SciShow Kids: "Animals with Winter Coats!"
https://www.youtube.com/watch?v=0N7FGPeykfE
This video showcases how animals use their coats to stay warm while living in frigid winter habitats.

PHOTO ACKNOWLEDGMENTS

Image credits: sirtravelalot/Shutterstock.com, p. 3; Neil Bromhall/Science Source, p. 4; Oscar Carrascosa Martinez/Shutterstock.com, p. 5; apiguide/Shutterstock.com, p. 6; Chris Stein/DigitalVision/Getty Images, p. 7; Arterra/UIG/Getty Images, p. 8 (left); Lina Keil/Shutterstock.com, p. 8 (middle); Jane Burton/Dorling Kindersley/Getty Images, p. 8 (right); Drakuliren/Shutterstock.com, p. 9; Ariel Celeste Photography/Shutterstock.com, p. 10; J. Lekavicius/Shutterstock.com, p. 11; Jukka Jantunen/Shutterstock.com, p. 12; Tom Brakefield/Stockbyte/Getty Images, p. 13; Loop Images/Universal Images Group/Getty Images, p. 14; Ignatiev Alexandr/Shutterstock.com, p. 15; ChrisVanLennepPhoto/Shutterstock.com, p. 16; michael sheehan/Shutterstock.com, p. 17; pkul/Shutterstock.com, p. 18; Nick Fox/Shutterstock.com, p. 19; Patrick Foto/Shutterstock.com, p. 20; wavebreakmedia/Shutterstock.com, p. 21; Everything I Do/Shutterstock.com, p. 22; Ivan Kuzmin/Shutterstock.com, p. 23; AltamashUrooj/Shutterstock.com, p. 24; Nivlac921/Shutterstock.com, p. 25 (left); Vishnevskiy Vasily/Shutterstock.com, p. 25 (right); Frans Lanting/Mint Images/Getty Images, p. 26; TatyanaPanova/Shutterstock.com, p. 27 (top); allanw/Shutterstock.com, p. 27 (bottom); vkilikov/Shutterstock.com, p. 28; Wild Horizon/UIG/Getty Images, p. 29; fantom_rd/Shutterstock.com, p. 30; Big Foot Productions/Shutterstock.com, p. 31; Rawpixel.com/Shutterstock.com, pp. 32 (top), 33; XiXinXing/Shutterstock.com, p. 32 (bottom). Design elements: Gorbash Varvara/Shutterstock.com; ivgroznii/Shutterstock.com.

Cover: GK Hart/Vikki Hart/DigitalVision/Getty Images; Kira Volkov/Shutterstock.com; WICHAI WONGJONGJAIHAN/Shutterstock.com; Only background/Shutterstock.com; Martin Harvey/Gallo Images/Getty Images.